Creation Creature Features
Wolves

For since the creation of the world God's invisible qualities—His eternal power and divine nature—have been clearly seen, being understood from what has been made, so that people are without excuse.

Romans 1:20

Wasil Science: Creation Creature Feature Series!
Wolves
By Joseph Wasil
Wasil Science, LLC.

From the Wasil Science Creation Creature Feature Series, Volume 48
© Copyright Wasil Science, LLC.

Let's explore God's incredible creation!

Millions of years ago…

This is where many science books begin, based on the idea that organisms evolved from nothing.
There is zero evidence scientifically to make such a claim.
We must look outside of nature for origins.
Nothingness can't create anything.
Somebody outside of nature created all things.
This is what we find in Genesis 1:1.
"In the beginning God created the heavens and the earth."

That same Creator, the Lord Almighty, designed the incredible WOLVES!

Check out this awesome wolf!

Wolves are amazing mammals designed by God to live in northern habitats!

These creatures are very intelligent and social as they live in groups called packs!

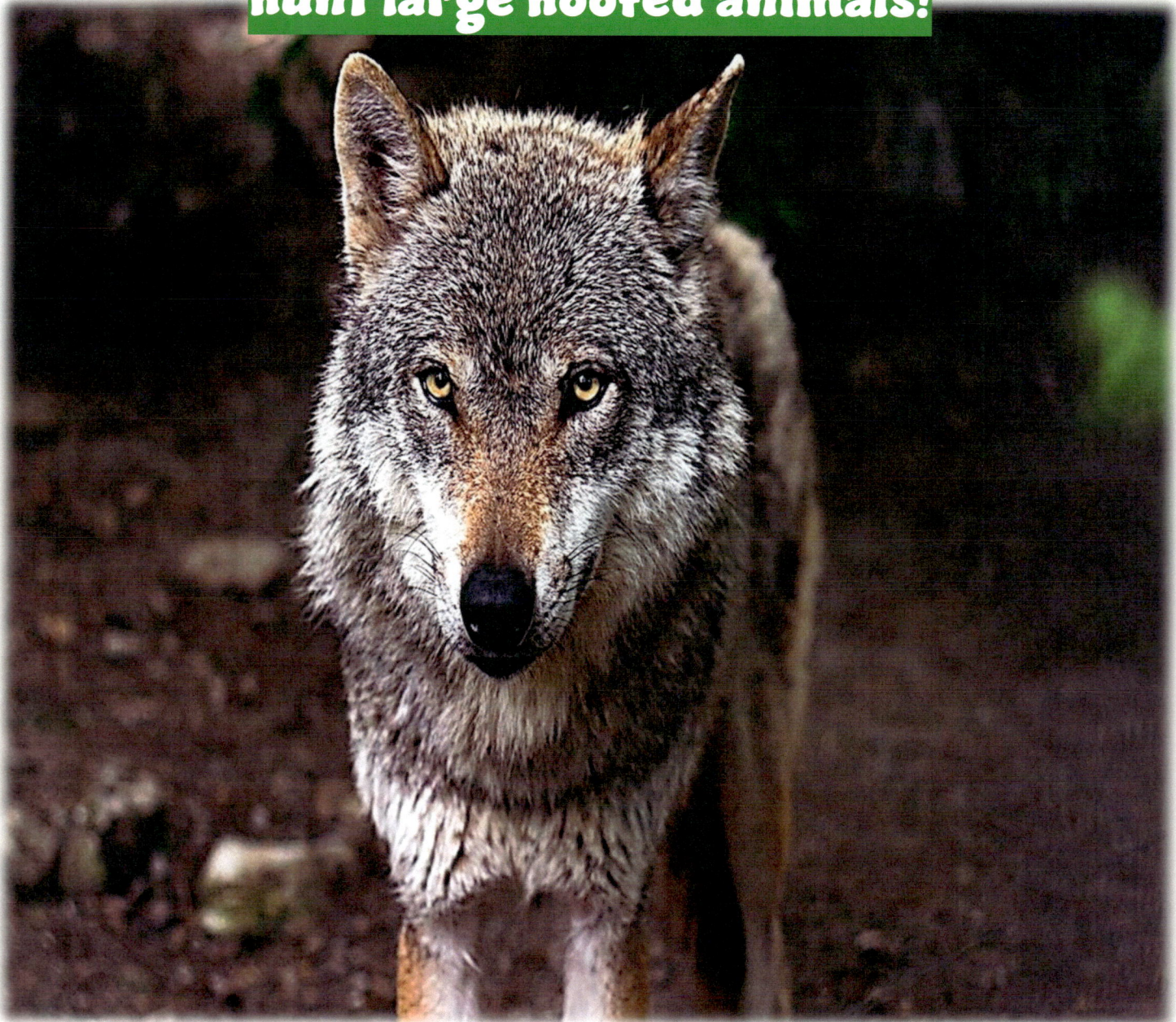

God designed the gray wolf to be the only member of the canine family to hunt large hoofed animals!

The menu for the wolf is deer and moose!

Wolves live up to 10 years in the wild.

God designed the gestation period to be about 63 days.

Mother wolves will usually give birth to about 5 young!

Check this out!
The body of the wolf is designed for stamina.

Wolves can cover over 35 miles a day when out hunting!

The skull of the wolf is designed to be large with strong teeth to grip and rip.

The large incisor teeth are designed to scrape muscle off the bone of prey!

God created wolves with an excellent sense of sight, smell, and hearing to track down prey!

Check out this amazing creation creature feature!

The thick fur of wolves is designed to keep warm and act as camouflage. While running wolves will often hold up their tail to help with stability!

Dominant males also hold their tail high to show strength.

Wolves grow to be about 5 feet long and can weigh over 170 pounds!

Wolves mate for life and will dig an underground den for young.

Wolves will track prey all day and night if needed.

Draw and color the habitat for the wolf!

God designed wolves to reach speeds of over 25 mph!

Their endurance ensures many successful hunts.

Wolf packs can include up to 10 members as they work together to survive in some harsh climates and habitats!

Thanks for joining us on this adventure of exploring God's incredible creation! Wolves are an amazing group of organisms designed by God. Each creature has interesting traits that makes them totally unique. From the smallest to the largest, every creature is created unique by our Lord Jesus!